MW01121701

MEASURING TEMPERATURE

⟶ Anne O'Daly ⟵

PowerKiDS
press™

Published in 2024 by The Rosen Publishing Group, Inc.
2544 Clinton Street, Buffalo, NY 14224

Portions of this work were originally authored by Chris Woodford and published as *Temperature*. All new material this edition authored by Anne O'Daly.

Children's Publisher: Anne O'Daly
Design Manager: Keith Davis
Picture Manager: Sophie Mortimer

Picture credits:

Key: t = top, tr = top right, b = bottom

Front Cover: Shutterstock: James Doss l, Somchai Som tr, Sliver Tiger tr, Christopher Wood main image.

Interior: iStock: Prill 17; Shutterstock: 4-5, 9, Igor Barin 21t, Barry Blackburn 10, Joe Balvao 12, BestPhotoStudio 26, Marcel Clemmens 16, courage007 14, grafvision 20, Gumbariya 8, Edward Haylan 24, neenwawat khenyothaa 6, Anna Maria Mejia 19, Olivier Le Moal 15, Puripat L. 13, SirTravellot 27, Julia Smile 7, Ivan Smuk 1, 22, Somchai Som 21, Phil Studio 11, Sliver Tiger 18, wimmamoth 5, H. N Xuan 21b.

All other artworks and photographs © Brown Bear Books.

Cataloging-in-Publication Data

Names: O'Daly, Anne.
Title: Measuring temperature / Anne O'Daly.
Description: New York : Powerkids Press, 2024. | Series: Measure it with math! | Includes glossary and index.
Identifiers: ISBN 9781642827859 (pbk.) | ISBN 9781642827866 (library bound) | ISBN 9781642827873 (ebook)
Subjects: LCSH: Temperature--Juvenile literature. | Temperature measurements--Juvenile literature.
Classification: LCC QC271.4 O34 2024 | DDC 536'.50287--dc23

Manufactured in the United States of America

CPSIA Compliance Information: Batch #CSPK24. For further information contact Rosen Publishing at 1-800-237-9932.

Find us on

Contents

What Is Temperature?

What's the weather like today? Is it warm and sunny? Is it snowy and cold? Temperature is a measure of how hot or cold something is. On a hot day, the temperature is high. On a cold day, the temperature is lower.

Measuring Temperature

We can measure temperature with a thermometer. This is an instrument that measures how hot or cold something is. A scale tells us the temperature. There are many different types of thermometers.

Snow falls when the air temperature is very low.

HEAT AND TEMPERATURE

Heat and temperature are not the same. Heat is a kind of energy. When a pan of soup is heated on a stove, the soup gets more energy. Heat energy makes the soup bubble and heat up. The soup has a high temperature because it is hot.

Measuring the temperature can be very useful. It tells us how hot the stove needs to be to cook our food. It helps us know if someone is healthy or ill. Knowing the temperature helps us decide what clothes to pack for a vacation.

Hot and Cold

It's easy to measure length. We can put a ruler next to a pencil and measure it. We cannot see temperature, but we can see how heat makes things change. Heat makes a metal bar grow longer. We can see that heat melts ice. We can also see how the sun dries up earth and makes it crack. A cup of hot chocolate feels warmer than a chocolate milkshake.

Hot weather makes water disappear from the ground. The soil gets very dry and cracks.

Changes

When things get hotter or colder, they change size. If we heat a metal bar, it gets a bit longer. When the bar cools down, it gets a bit shorter. If we could measure how long the bar was when it was hot and cold, the length could tell us something about its temperature.

Water, Ice, and Steam

Water can help us measure temperature. When water is very cold, it freezes to make solid ice. At everyday temperatures, water is a liquid. When we heat water, it turns into a gas called steam.

Icicles form when drops of water freeze and turn into ice.

How thermometers Work

One type of thermometer is a hollow tube made of glass. Inside the tube is a liquid. The liquid can be mercury or alcohol. Mercury looks like a thin silver line inside the glass. Alcohol looks like a thin red line. The tube has numbers marked along its side. This is the scale. It tells us what the temperature is.

A digital thermometer is safer to use than a mercury thermometer.

FACT

Mercury is poisonous. Many countries and states have banned mercury thermometers for sale for use in people's homes.

Mercury is a metal. Most metals are solid at everyday temperatures, but mercury is a liquid. It moves up and down a thermometer. Even a small temperature change makes the mercury move. Alcohol thermometers work in the same way. The top of the line shows the temperature.

The answer is on page 32.

What temperature is this? ——————

liquid line ——————

alcohol —————— (colored red)

bulb ——————

°C °F

°C	°F
50	120
40	100
30	80
20	60
10	40
0	20
10	20
20	0
30	20

Heating Up, Cooling Down

When the tip of the thermometer touches something, heat energy passes to the liquid inside. When the liquid gets hot, it takes up more space. This makes it move up the tube. When it cools down, it moves down the tube.

Reading the Scale

The mercury or alcohol moves up and down inside the glass tube as the temperature changes. The liquid moves along the scale. We can find the temperature by seeing where the liquid line is on the scale. When the liquid moves down the scale, the temperature around us is lower than when it moves up the scale.

Scales and Units

We measure temperature in units called degrees. The numbers on a thermometer's scale show how many degrees the temperature is. A high temperature could be hundreds or thousands of degrees. A low temperature might be just a few degrees. Degrees have their own symbol. We write it like this: °

Fahrenheit

Thermometers have different scales. In the United States, the most common scale is the Fahrenheit scale. On this scale, water boils at a temperature of 212 degrees. We write this as 212°F. The "F" shows that we are using the Fahrenheit scale.

The numbers around the thermometer show the temperature in Fahrenheit.

Cold Freeze

When water gets very cold, it freezes and turns into ice. The temperature of freezing water is 32 degrees Fahrenheit, or 32°F. Colder temperatures can measure 0°F on the Fahrenheit scale. Even colder temperatures can go below zero. The coldest temperatures on Earth are in Antarctica, around the South Pole. Temperatures there are below 0 degrees Fahrenheit.

The numbers on the right of the thermometer show the temperature in Fahrenheit.

FACT

The coldest-ever temperature on Earth was −128.6 degrees Fahrenheit. It was measured in Antarctica in 1983.

Celsius Scale

Distances can be measured in feet and inches or in centimeters and meters. Feet and inches are part of the imperial system. Centimeters and meters are metric. In the same way, there are different temperature scales. The Celsius scale is linked to the metric system. It is used in most countries in the world. The Celsius scale is measured in degrees. On the Celsius scale, water freezes at 0 degrees. We write this as 0° Celsius, or 0°C.

Some towns have boards that show the temperature.

CHANGING BETWEEN FAHRENHEIT AND CELSIUS

If you know a temperature in Fahrenheit, you can figure out what it is in Celsius.

1. Subtract 32 from the Fahrenheit temperature.

$$212°F - 32 = 180$$

2. Then multiply the answer by 5.

$$180 × 5 = 900$$

3. Next, divide you answer by 9.

$$900 / 9 = 100$$

So 212°F is the same as 100°C.

You can also change Celsius to Fahrenheit.

1. First multiply the Celsius temperature by 9.

$$100°C × 9 = 900$$

2. Then divide the answer by 5.

$$900 / 5 = 180$$

3. Next, add 32 to your answer.

$$180 + 32 = 212$$

So 100°C is the same as 212°F.

What is 50°F in degrees Celsius? The answer is on page 32.

Boiling Water

Water boils at a temperature of 100 degrees on the Celsius scale. We write this as 100°. To show we are using the Celsius scale, we write 100° Celsius or 100°C for short. Celsius is sometimes called centigrade. The two are the same. So 100 degrees centigrade is the same as 100 degrees Celsius.

A hot spring in Iceland sends out a jet of boiling water and steam.

Digital thermometers

Digital thermometers have a computer chip inside them. The tip of the thermometer can sense temperature. When it touches an object, it measures the temperature. It sends it to the computer chip. The temperature shows on a screen. Digital thermometers are used to take people's temperature when they are ill.

Large digital thermometers on the outside of buildings measure the air temperature. Digital thermometers are used in kitchens and restaurants. They measure the temperature of food to make sure it is properly cooked.

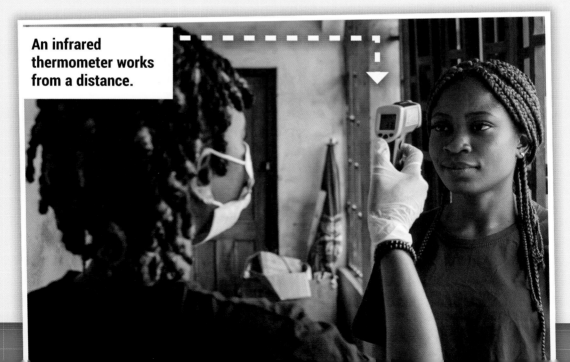

An infrared thermometer works from a distance.

ON OR OFF?

A thermostat controls the temperature of a room or house. It measures the temperature in the room at the time. The temperature shows on a screen. If the temperature gets too high, the thermostat switches off the heater. If the temperature is too low, the thermostat switches the heat on again.

If the thermostat is set at 65°F and the room temperature is 60°F, will the thermostat switch the heat on or off? What will happen if the room temperature is 70°F?

Answers on page 32.

FACT

Some thermometers use sound to measure temperature! Hot objects give out sound waves, which the thermometers can pick up.

From a Distance

Infrared thermometers are a type of digital thermometer. They measure temperature from a distance. They work from a few inches or a few miles. Infrared temperatures are used when it isn't safe to get too close to the object. They were used during the COVID-19 pandemic to take people's temperature without touching them.

First thermometers

Italian scientist Galileo invented the first thermometer in 1592. It was an upside-down glass jar filled with water and air. His instrument could show temperature differences but it didn't measure them. Later scientists added a scale to the thermometer and tried different substances inside.

Mercury Thermometer

Daniel Fahrenheit was a German scientist.
In 1714, he decided to use mercury in a thermometer.
Fahrenheit also worked out a temperature scale.
He used the freezing points and boiling points
of water. The Fahrenheit scale is still used today.

Daniel Fahrenheit used mercury in his thermometer. Mercury is the only metal that is liquid at room temperature.

THERMOSCOPE

Galileo's thermometer was called a thermoscope. Galileo took a round jar with a long glass neck and warmed it. Then he turned the jar upside down. He dipped the neck into a bowl of water. The air in the jar cooled and shrank a little. That pulled some of the water from the bowl up the glass neck.

This thermometer is based on Galileo's thermoscope. It has glass bubbles floating in water. The lowest bubble tells us what the temperature is.

FACT

In 1612, Italian doctor Santorio Santorio added numbers to a thermometer. He used it on his patients to see if they had a fever.

The Celsius Scale

In 1742, Swedish scientist Anders Celsius invented another temperature scale. He chose 0 degrees for the boiling point of water and 100 degrees for the freezing point. Later, scientists turned the scale the other way up. This is the Celsius or centigrade scale.

How Low Can You Go?

Everything in the universe is made of tiny particles called atoms. Atoms join together to make molecules. When something gets hot, its molecules move around. The hotter it gets, the faster the molecules move. The colder something is, the slower its molecules move.

HOT, HOTTER, HOTTEST!

Absolute zero is the lowest temperature anything can reach. But no one really knows what the hottest temperature could be. The hottest temperature ever recorded on Earth is 134°F (56.7°C). That was in Death Valley in California. The temperature inside the sun is about 25 million °F!

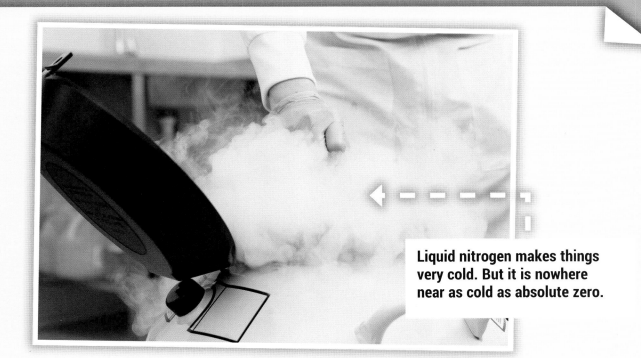

Liquid nitrogen makes things very cold. But it is nowhere near as cold as absolute zero.

What would happen if something got so cold that its molecules stopped moving altogether? That temperature is called absolute zero. It's the same as -460 degrees on the Fahrenheit scale and -273 degrees on the Celsius scale. Absolute zero is the coldest possible temperature.

Kelvin Scale

The Kelvin scale is mainly used by scientists.
It has absolute zero as the lowest point of the scale.
The Kelvin scale uses the letter K but doesn't have the degree sign. So 10 degrees on the Kelvin scale is 10 K.

the Colors of Heat

When you watch a fire, the flames flicker yellow and red. Lots of things change color when they heat up. If we heat an iron bar in a furnace, it slowly changes color.

Changing Color

First the iron bar turns a red-brown. As it gets hotter, it glows red, orange, and yellow. Finally, it turns white. The iron turns red at about 1,750°F (954°C). A yellow-hot bar is around 2,000°F (1,093°C).

Blacksmiths use the color of metal to tell them when it is hot and soft enough to shape.

LIGHT

Some hot things give out light as well as heat. Most light bulbs have a thin piece of wire inside them. The wire gets very hot and gives out heat and light energy. When hot things give out light, we know they are very hot indeed.

Working with Color

Blacksmiths make things from metal. They know they can only shape metal when it is very hot. Blacksmiths heat metal until it glows orange-red. Then they know it is hot enough to bend and hammer into shape.

Seeing Heat

Special cameras can see heat instead of light. They are thermal cameras. Hot objects give off invisible rays called infrared radiation. Thermal cameras pick up this radiation and turn it into a picture. Hotter areas show in a different color to colder areas. It is easy to see which parts are hot.

A thermal camera shows the places where houses are losing heat. The red areas are hottest, and the blue areas are coldest.

24.2

3.1

Thermal cameras can help our homes save energy. They show the parts of the house where most heat escapes. We can insulate those areas to keep our homes warmer. This saves money, and helps save the planet by using less energy.

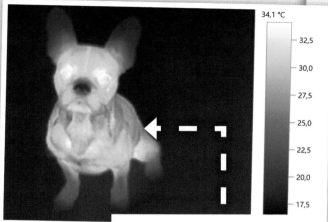

A thermal image of a French bulldog. It has a hot body, cooler ears and paws, and a cold nose!

Body Heat

Thermal pictures help us see in the dark. Our bodies give off heat. Thermal cameras help rescue teams find people who are lost at night. The camera can "see" the person's body heat, even in the dark. We can also use thermal cameras to photograph animals that come out at night.

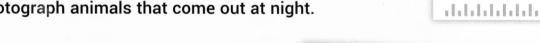

SNAKES

Some snakes can pick up infrared radiation. Sense organs on the snake's face pick up heat from other animals. This helps the snake hunt prey, even in the dark. It also helps them avoid predators that might hunt snakes!

Weather Forecast

Measuring temperature helps us forecast the weather. Earth's weather is mainly caused by the sun. The sun sends heat energy to Earth. That makes Earth warm up.

During the year, different parts of our planet have more hours of sunlight than others. When the sun is higher in the sky, its rays are stronger and warmer. Different parts of our planet warm up by different amounts. They have different temperatures. That is what causes weather.

A weather balloon measures the temperature high up in the sky.

TRY THIS

CLIMATE CHART

We can see what kind of climate a place has by looking at a chart of its temperature. The high bars show warmer months. The low bars show cooler ones. Looking at the chart tells us the temperature at different times of the year.

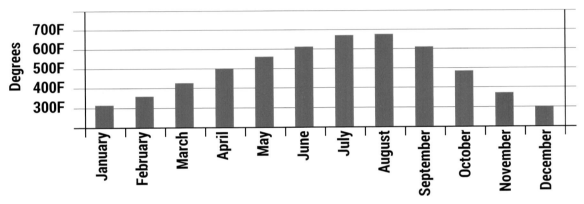

What temperature is it:
In April? In August? In December?

Answers on page 32.

Weather is what happens over a short time. Climate is the pattern of weather over a year. Some places are hot all year round. Others have months of warm weather and months of cold weather.

25

temperature and Life

Animals need a temperature that is just right for them. If the temperature is too hot or too cold, they may get sick and even die.

Cold-blooded
Fish, snakes, and lizards are cold-blooded animals. They cannot make their own body heat. To heat up, a cold-blooded animal sits in a sunny spot. It basks in the sun until it is warm enough to get active. To cool down, it moves somewhere less hot.

A crocodile basks in the sun. Crocodiles are cold-blooded animals. They get their heat from their surroundings.

Warm-Blooded

Birds and mammals are warm-blooded. They make their own body heat. They get energy from food. That warms them from the inside. Feathers and fur keep them warm when the weather is cold.

Dogs are warm-blooded. They make their own body heat. They stick out their tongue and pant when they get too warm.

BODY TEMPERATURE

Doctors take people's temperature to find out if they are ill. A person's body temperature is normally 98.6°F (37°C). If a person is sick, their body temperature goes up. Ask an adult to measure your temperature with a medical thermometer. How close are you to normal body temperature?

Estimating temperature

WHAT YOU NEED

* Liquid-crystal thermometer strips
* A pencil and paper
* Things to test

WHAT TO DO

1. Think of some things around your home that you can test. You might test:

A sunny part of a room

Your arm

A cold faucet

Different materials, such as paper, metal, or wood

Liquid Crystal

A liquid–crystal thermometer is a plastic strip. It has a special liquid in pockets. The pockets have numbers printed on them. As the temperature rises, the liquid in the pockets changes color. A number appears on the pocket. That number is the temperature.

°F	95	96.8	98.6	100.4	102.2	104
°C	35	36	37	38	39	40

2. Write down the names of the items on the paper.

3. Touch each one in turn. Does it feel hot or cold? Compare the items on your list.

4. List the items from hottest to coldest, based on how they felt.

5. Now place a liquid-crystal thermometer strip on each of the objects.

6. Wait a few minutes for the temperature to settle. Then read the temperature on the strip.

7. Write down the temperature next to each item on the list.

8. Look again to see the order, from hottest to coldest. Did you figure out the order correctly?

Glossary

absolute zero The lowest temperature that can ever be reached.

atom A very small piece of a substance.

body temperature The normal temperature of a person, 98.6°F (37°C).

Celsius A temperature scale figured out by Anders Celsius. Also called the centigrade scale.

centigrade A temperature scale based on the temperatures of ice and boiling water. Also called the Celsius scale.

climate The weather a place has over the course of a period of time.

degree A single unit of temperature.

digital thermometer A thermometer that shows the temperature in numbers.

energy The ability of something to do work.

Fahrenheit A temperature scale figured out by Daniel Fahrenheit.

filament A thin wire that produces light when heated.

geyser A natural fountain of steam and very hot water.

heat A type of energy that makes something hot or cold.

Kelvin A temperature scale that starts at absolute zero.

mercury A metal that was used inside thermometers.

molecule A group of joined atoms.

scale Marks on a thermometer that help us measure.

steam The gas formed when water is heated to 212°F (100°C).

temperature A measurement of how hot or cold something is.

thermal image A kind of photograph that shows areas of heat.

thermometer An instrument for measuring temperature.

thermostat A device that switches heaters on or off to keep a room at the right temperature.

Find Out More

BOOKS

Amstutz, Lisa J.
Thermometers.
Capstone Publishing, 2020.

Coates, Eileen S.
*The Temperature Scales
of Fahrenheit and Celsius*.
Rosen Publishing, 2019.

Rustad, Martha E. H.
Measuring Temperature.
Capstone Publishing, 2019.

Tomecek, Steve.
All About Heat Waves and Droughts.
Children's Press, 2021.

WEBSITES

www.bbc.co.uk/bitesize/topics/zc3g87h/
articles/znw7jsg
Lots of information about heating and
cooling.

www.mathsisfun.com/temperature-
conversion.html
How to convert all kinds of
temperatures from imperial to metric.

thepolesworthschool.com/wp-content/
uploads/2020/06/KS3-Year-8-Science-
Independent-Learning-Booklets-Heating-
and-Cooling.pdf
A booklet with explanations,
illustrations, exercises, games,
puzzles, and quizzes about heating
and temperature.

Index

ANSWERS

Page 9: 30C (or about 86F). **Page 13:** 10C. **Page 15:** On; Off. **Page 25:** 500F, 680F, and 300F.